For our friends

Third printing 2018

Whoof!

My name is Amadeus, and this book is to help my master with his sadness because I have died. It is also help to you to succeed at school.

He has been a good master, and I love him very much. I first came into his life as a puppy, only five and a half years ago, and we have been together all this time. We have also had some real adventures together, which are also in this book I am writing with him for you.

I know nothing about mathematics. I expect you are the same.

But I know that when he was teaching, he didn't just want his pupils to remember his instructions. He realized this was making them dislike and even hate each other. It was hurting them.

He wanted to help them learn how to think for themselves!

How to do this puzzled him for a long time. Until he made an amazing discovery! Most amazing because it has have obvious for very long time. Probably important people just didn't want any to notice it, because it makes them much less important!

You are going to find out about his discovery as you work through our book. It will help you not just to enjoy learning mathematics, but to enjoy learning everything that you will ever want to learn.

More than this: you will learn how to learn together with your class, so that you all stay liking each other and become more confident in yourselves. You will not be made to believe that others are more intelligent or less intelligent than you are.

Being intelligent is about being so confident of yourself that you can be kind to everyone around you. This is what really matters.

You don't need to boast about being strong.

All puppies learn this. Being strong doesn't mean be able to frighten everyone. It means there is nothing that can frighten you.

This will be obvious.

Enjoy my adventures and lessons. I learnt something new in every one of them! You will too.

Best wishes from Amadeus!

Here's the place for your name:

....

and also your school:

....

Here is my first lesson: How a human brain works!

Your yooman brain is very different from mine. My dog brain is very good at listening and sniffing and understanding sounds and smells!

Yours is more complicated.

Press your two fists together in front of you, and let me explain.

Your fists are almost exactly the shape and size of your brain.

You should be surprised. But it has to fit, up there! Try it!

Your right fist is the right side of your brain. It it is very good at learning habits. All the habits you have ever learnt are in here.

Many people learn all the habits they need to learn as they are growing up. They may never need to learn any more more. If it's hot enough, they may not even need clothes. Like me!

The right side of everyone's brain is *very* emotional.

It can make you feel happy, or weepy, or angry.

Most of all, if anyone tries to question any of its habits, like saying it could be wrong, it will get *very very angry*!

This is why grown-ups often try to kill each other. They think another is criticising their habits of believing or behaving, and they cannot allow this to happen. So they try to kill them.

Only the left side of your brain is entirely yooman. Only this side can speak, listen, compare the result of one habit and another, and persuade the right side to change without getting it angry!

It has taken yoomans a very long time to learn how to do this. Little children still get very very angry - and noisy!- if they aren't given the treat they were expecting. Have you seen them? Heard them?

Now remember when you were trying to do something which has always worked before, and it failed. You said "Pish!" - or something similar - and tried something different.

It was your right brain that said "Pish!" Then your left brain tried something different. You may even have said what you next tried to do. This was the left side telling the right side the habit had to be changed.

This is an important clue! When I do something the master doesn't like, he doesn't hit me. He never has! He only tries to persuade me, quietly, not to wee on the policeman's leg, who wasn't looking, or - much more loudly - that I was wrong to steal the BEEF TOMATO from the greengrocer's display. He didn't notice I had it until we got home.

Then I ate it. I can read 'BEEF', but had a very odd taste!

The next day the master had to go back to pay for it.

In Primary School you learn almost everything as habits.

But after Primary School it will be very hard to learn anything new unless you learn to change habits without getting angry with yourself. Or your teacher.

Next is to learn to accept being told that others disagree with you, without you getting angry with them!

Next is to learn how to tell others that you disagree with them, without being angry or getting them angry with you!

This is often why there is so much trouble in class. Many children have just never learnt what you have just learnt.

Their right brain is out of control!

When people show that they are angry, it is their right brain that is angry. If you try to tell a right brain that it is WRONG , what will happen?

It will just get EVEN ANGRIER!

Their right brain will get COMPLETELY OUT OF CONTROL!

Fortunately you have a powerful left brain to help you.

And, although it may not work as well, so have they.

The solution is to get them to turn away from the anger in their right brain, and start listening with the left.

You must do the same.

You and your class must learn to argue WITHOUT ANGER.

And the best place to do this,

                    IS A MATHEMATICS LESSON!!!

Here comes my first adventure. With the Mud Monster. This was first written by the master for his own pupils. He can't write like me. Whoof!

Amadeus and the Mud Monster.

Although it was certainly alarming to have fallen into the garden pond at a very early age, Amadeus has since learnt to have no fear of swimming. In fact, having recently discovered, to his own surprise, that he can sometimes even walk - in another adventure, *on* water - he is usually ready to jump into any lake, river, or stream.

A few days ago, the day being unusually hot, he was eager to get to the far side of the meadow and into a stream that runs there, in a deep gulley hidden by head-high thickets of - mainly - nettles from the sight of anyone else on the meadow and from the road beyond.

I should have noticed that the water level in the stream had fallen several feet, leaving a three-foot vertical bank. Having splashed about happily for several minutes, when Amadeus tried to pull himself out again, as he had previously with ease, his front paws only carved deep grooves in the fudge-soft earth, whilst his back paws could get no purchase at all.

After several minutes of this hopeless activity, he was beginning to get desperate; getting ever muddier, barking eventually in frustration, and eventually howling: "WOOOHOOOHOOH!"

By now the water around him is a boiling black soup, as his frantic churning releases an eruption of methane gas from the mud, the bursting bubbles bringing with them a vile stench and masses of decayed black leaf and broken twigs.

He is soon festooned with this stinking black muck as well, even to his ears; but, still, whenever I tried to reach him to pull him out - the bank being both steep and slippery - the silly mutt would only rear back, barking - at me! - even more furiously.

Eventually I was able to get hold of his collar. Ahah!

He jerks back. I have pulled his collar right off his head! Before, this situation was just a nuisance. Now there is a real problem. There is now nothing to catch hold of except his coat. But at one-and-not-yet-one-half-a-year old, the puppy, known as Amadeus, weighs well over a hundred pounds. Wet, as he now is: even more. Nor is he in a mood to co-operate. He will very likely bite, as dogs do when sufficiently frightened. I judged this situation to be perfectly sufficient.

Now is therefore the time for a calm - a very calm - Appreciation of the Situation: as I was taught, with just these Capitals, in my military training.

The most obvious and sensible military option is to walk away and let the silly idiot find a way out by himself. The other, not-so-very-sensible military, option is to get into the damned stream with him.

I sighed. I was, for a change, quite nicely dressed. I was wearing clean summer slacks, my Socrates T-shirt (on which that noble philosopher is drinking his hemlock: how very appropriate!), and my beautiful new, ridiculously expensive, Asic gel-cushioned trainers, in which finally I was able to walk a little less like Quasimodo.

I had the sense, at least, to place my specs on the bank and out of harm's way. Then I dropped into the water. Hah! Not just water. This was a foot of water and then feet, feet, fee-eet, fee-ee-eet of soft deep mud.

By now Amadeus was now swimming around behind me in circles, apparently relieved that I have joined the fun. As in all fraught moments, time slows down.

The sinking stops when the water is at my waist. Very carefully, I transfer my weight to my left foot. It sinks deeper. Now I try to lift the right.

Hmm. It will not move at all. I know that I am not really being 'sucked down' - as heroines tend to shriek in movies. Mud, I calmly tell myself - not alarmed at all - has more buoyancy than water. I cannot sink forever. But I may still drown. I imagine myself embalmed in mud, like that old guy found years ago in a Northern bog.

The water has now crept up high on my chest. Decision time.

I lie back in the stream - it is surprisingly tepid - and wait for my ridiculously expensive trainers, now ruined, to be released. After a long pause, this happens, and I am able to set off, partly swimming, partly - yes! - dog-paddling up-stream to find a section of sloping bank up which we might both be able to crawl.

It was now, I later realized, that Amadeus showed true intelligence. The only real fear that I had was that he would decide to use me as a convenient raft and climb onto me. This is what many dogs would do; and this would have been extremely nasty, for I had no firm bottom under me. I did not want to drown with lungs full of mud. Despite all the hullabaloo he had made earlier, no-one had come to investigate. We were hidden on both sides by the tall weeds. I would drown unseen.

To my relief, Amadeus did not try to use me as a raft, but kept swimming companionably up-stream with me. On both sides the overgrown banks remained vertical; the weeds hiding us; no hope; no hope. And then: salvation!

The mass of roots of an old willow tree showed as a tangle looking like red wires in the black earth: a tangle into which Amadeus could fix his claws.

Without attempting any explanation of what we were about to do, I pulled him to me, pushed him up against this web, and as his claws caught hold - such a clever pup - got my shoulder under his bum - and PUSHED!

Up he went, with a yelp of satisfaction. Then it's my turn. I am sodden. I weigh much more than a hundred pounds, and I am not as spry as I used to be. Fortunately, old willow trees have deeply fissured bark. Although big chunks kept breaking off in my hands - and watched,

I think anxiously, by Amadeus - I find a thick ivy strand that would not break, and pulled myself out.

And then only to push through all the bloody nettles.

Ouch, ouch, ouch!

But, come on! No leeches; no snakes; no clouds of mosquitoes. Out in the sun-drenched and still deserted meadow again, I stripped off all my mud-soddened clothes to sit naked on my fisherman's seat to dry. What an adventure. I find that I have wrenched my left shoulder climbing out.

WHUMP! A wet hundred pound puppy lands on my back; his paws on my shoulders, he snorts in my hair. Amadeus is thanking his saviour. Charging round and round in circles, he finally launched himself at me again. I am embraced, enthusiastically, violently, and passionately. "We won! We won!!"

I am left with a long bloody scratch on one fore arm. This could have been made by the willow bark - and not by him. But, again, anyone who doesn't have a sense of humour should never have a dog!

Stop laughing! Next is my Second Lesson.

My Second Lesson : RESPECT

Showing respect is very important to us dogs. If we disrespect our mum, she will growl, then may give us a nip. If really annoyed, she will bite us. If she is pleased, she will give us a lick.

We learn respect from her care.

Other dogs show their respect by approaching us slowly, and by wagging their tails. This sends us their scent, which tells us nearly everything we need to know. The stronger dog then shows his respect by beginning to wag his tail. If the other dog doesn't show us enough respect, we must fight him 'til one of us loses.

You yoomans behave much the same. Does the other yooman look same? Act the same? Talk the same? You have the biggest problems with what they believe. Showing disrespect for anyone's habit of believing is about the worst thing you can do.

So how can you learn not to do this? You need to find a way to show your respect by arguing with others of your age about something they will not get upset about! What can that be?

You will be expected in your school to learn mathematics for years and years. It is all about things, like numbers. It's also nothing but argument. How best to do this. How best to do that.

This is just what everyone's left brain likes to do!

How many ways do you know to make others angry? Laughing at them. Sneering at them. Ignoring them.

This has to stop.

In my next lesson I will show you how you can argue about mathematics for ever without upsetting anyone. You may even invent new ways to do things that no one has thought of before.

And how you may get your teachers to help!

Next is one my favourites: The story of the Exploding Egg!

Amadeus and the Easter Surprise.

Amadeus has had an interest in eggs ever since I rolled the first he ever saw in his life across the floor to him at breakfast.

It *was* hard-boiled, and nearly cold. He was lying in one of his then favourite positions, on his belly on the old rag rug by the sofa.

This first egg wobbled across the tiled floor towards him, as eggs given some impetus do, and stopped an inch from his nose.

Amadeus stared at for a longish time, obviously thinking: *'I've never seen anything like this before; it moves without legs; it could be dangerous'.*

When it failed to surprise him further, he gave it a cautious nudge.

It wobbled away a few inches, and stopped again. It was obviously trying escape: even without legs.

He gave it another nudge, then another, and then another, creeping after it on his belly until he and his egg had moved all the way across the floor until it came to a stop against the wall.

Now it could move no further.

Amadeus thought about this for another longish while. He had proved it was no threat. It was even rather cowardly. It couldn't stand and fight.

Finally he stretched out his right leg, and slapped it, hard.

Eggshells are actually extremely strong. Take an egg in your hand and subject it to a steady pressure, and I am sure that you will be impressed.

If you are brave enough, try a not boiled egg!

Although Amadeus was only then a few months old, the paw with which he hit the egg was already almost as big and almost as heavy as my own hand.

He squashed his egg almost flat. Its shell split open. Inside the white split as well, revealing the round yoke like a small orange sun.

He gave the white a cautious sniff, then the yoke a lick. Hmm. It's good!

And it was doomed. He scooped out the yoke and ate it. Then he ate the white. Then he ate the shell. And his first egg was gone.

From that day on Amadeus' mastery of the egg steadily improved. He discovered that you don't actually need to slap eggs around. Just pick up your egg gently with your teeth, lift the head high, then drop it. Splat! Then, eat. Simple!

Amadeus also learnt that the tiled floor does the business perfectly. Then they split more easily and there are no growls from above about staining the rug.

One of our favourite sites to explore is called Tumbling Bay Pool.

It was once a public swimming pool, built, I imagine, in the 1950s.

Most people are today discouraged from swimming *au naturel*, and it is now rarely visited, it. Far from the public eye: it is secluded, being surrounded by a close-linked fence; while the pool itself is now hugely overgrown with tall green reeds growing from the deep mud (more mud!) on its floor.

Although now neglected, its concrete tank and footpaths remain sound; and the water from the Thames (the Isis in Oxford) flows over the upper weir with a delightful rush into the swimming pool, and lower down flows, not unnaturally, over another weir and out again. A rough but still very substantial wooden bridge crosses it in the middle.

This, as you will recognize, is where Amadeus first found that he can walk on water. Here he is also discovering, as Xerxes proved, that you can't frighten water by shouting at it. Xerxes, you remember, ordered the disobedient sea to be whipped.

On this particular day, shortly after Easter, there were only two men fishing in the pool itself, and they greeted, first Amadeus, who made himself known to them in his usual ebullient fashion, then me, in a very friendly way, and assured us - or me - that we could not possibly frighten their fish, because there weren't any; but this was better than being at home, where their wives wanted them to be decorating.

They were called Tim and Mick, and they chatted happily with me whilst Amadeus went exploring. He spent some time at first barking at the waterfall, then trying to eat it; but when this excitement palled, he jumped up onto the concrete buttress of the overgrown eyot you can see behind him, where he disappeared into the bushes which had fifty years of neglect had allowed to grow there.

Tim and Mick and I were continuing our analysis of our government's grasp of international cultural and political relations: *"These ---- fish,"* said Tim, *"have got more sense!"*; then clearly feeling that his alliteration lent more authority to his argument was saying this again, when there arose a tremendous clatter of wings from the hidden side of the eyot, accompanied by a storm of enraged squawking. *"Coo,"* said Mick, *"E's frightened them ducks."*

We never saw them ducks, but it sounded as if Amadeus had set an entire angry squadron in flight. Presently, however, very much like an opera diva parting the curtain to deliver her grand finale, he emerged from the eyot, his head held high in triumph, holding in his jaws a ball. It was a large grey ball.

"E's found an old ball," said Mick. *"Tennis."*

But it was a very strange old tennis ball. As Amadeus splashed proudly across the weir to jump out on the other side from us, we could now see his find more clearly. *"That's norra ball,"* said Tim. *"He's found a negg!"*

And now we could better understand Amadeus' pride. He was carrying an uncommonly large grey egg. Despite all the squawking, far too big to be a duck egg.

It was a goose egg.

The young pirate Amadeus, all alone and unsupported, had found, had conquered, and plundered the nest of a very large goose nest: of some very large geese, of the kind that spends much the summer up-stream on Port Meadow, and was now walking across the water of the weir to enjoy his plunder on terra firma.

By now - as you know - Amadeus knows that eggs do not peel themselves. Eggs must be cracked. Watched, with bated breath, by his audience of three, the fish, absent or not, entirely forgotten, Amadeus took his beautiful big goose egg behind the remaining bench on the other side of the pool, lifted it high, high, high! - and dropped it smartly onto the bare concrete.

And it exploded:

"BANG!"

"Christ!" said Tim. *"Jesus!"* said Mick, no less piously.

A thin blue smoke was curling above the site of his exploded egg, around its broken shell was spreading a horrid vomitous yellow pool.

The poor pirate Amadeus was thunderstruck. No egg had *ever* done that before. All his courage had been in vain.

And you, dear readers, may suppose that I have exercised a little dramatic license here: that his egg just went "Pop!" Or you might possibly allow: "POP!"

No, no, no, and again no. This egg exploded with a report like a forty-four calibre handgun in telephone box. Try imagining that. It should make your ears ring.

Tim and Mick and I abandoned our analysis of the international relations to try to imagine how long that piece of unexploded ordnance had been waiting for an inexperienced dog, or child, to pick it up. At least a year we thought; even two.

"It don't bear thinking about," said Tim.

"You wouldn't want one of them going off in your 'and," said Mick.

"Or in yer car," added Tim. *"Ugh!"*

We all agreed that *'Ugh'*, pretty well covered all these eventualities, as well as others that we had not had time to think of.

But neither of us had thought to keep on an eye on the pirate Amadeus, or - not to confuse matter too much - an eye on his eyot.

And it was now, from that dangerous corner of fair England, that there came a a heavy thud; a thud rather like this: "**THUD**!": a thud, believe me, of exactly the tone and timbre of an eighty millimetre mortar being fired from its tube, a sound to chill the blood of any soldier. Is that theirs, or is it ours? Its bomb is already a thousand feet up; now it's arching over; in another few seconds it will explode in a shower of white-hot shrapnel a hundred feet above the ground. Seconds to live.

This time, I will grant you, the mortar was half a mile away; but the sound was unmistakeably of deadly import. Then a silence: no more squawking; silence.

"God," breathed Tim. *"E's found another one!"*

"Oh, I do hope not," whispered Mick.

Even in this awful silence, I found myself feeling grateful for the honest concern of these two gentle men.

But before I could utter my own prayer for his safety, Amadeus suddenly appeared again on his eyot.

This time he came out backwards. No longer the pirate chief: no more the opera star: more a rather worried looking puppy. He crossed the weir for the last time, head down, tail down, too dispirited even to take a parting stab at the waterfall.

Amadeus learnt a lesson that day that I doubt he will ever forget. It must be something like this: 'Never trust an egg: especially an Easter egg. Some of them are made to explode!'

That was a lesson I'll never forget. My next is how to involve your friends – and your teacher!'

My Third Lesson: More is better!

Your right brain is a threat to peace in the classroom. Only your left brain can think clearly; can listen to other ideas, and can compare them with its own; can discuss them without anger; can persuade your right brain to change or replace habits without a tantrum.

Only your left brain is fully yooman.

But it does need time to think.

Which is why it is much better not to try to learn thinking and arguing alone, but with the help of a whole class. And a teacher.

All teachers deserve your respect.

They are generally supposed to get a whole class to think as they do. This is impossible. It is disastrous for the teacher.

But this is why they are always asking questions like: "Do you all understand?" This is disastrous for the class.

It will soon be divided into three groups. Each hating the others.

There will be a few who think they do. Most will be too frightened to say that they don't. The rest will know that they don't. They are beginning to feel abandoned. The majority will hope that they will be able to 'catch up' later. They may not.

But they all say that they do. They begin to suspect that the teacher know this is not true. Then that he knows that they know he knows it is not true. They lose their respect for that teacher. They stop respecting each other. The few will decide that the others are all stupid. The majority will decide that to appear to succeed, they must learn to be successfully dishonest: and that anyone who can't to this is lazy or too stupid. The rest believe everyone is lying.

A good teacher will want to help all his pupils to learn to think.

This isn't so difficult. In fact, it is great fun. For everyone.

But teaching has to be organized in a very new way.

Start by giving this book to a teacher you trust. After a time, ask for just one Amadeus lesson a month.

Just as a trial. For fun!

Make it a success!.

This will give you and the teacher more confidence.

The lesson has to be with a textbook.

Best is a textbook in mathematics with lots of explanations to read, lots of examples, and questions. Less silly pictures.

With only some help from your teacher, you and your class are going to learn how to learn from this textbook.

By reading this textbook you are going to learn all you need to go on to the next level, and the next, and the next.

HERE IS HOW AN AMADEUS LESSON WORKS!

"Open your book," your teacher will say, "at page so-and-so. We are now going to learn to understand an explanation of such-and-such."

The teacher will ask someone to read aloud a first sentence from that explanation.

This must be read ALOUD.

The teacher will still ask, "Has everyone heard?"

If any shake their head, "Then you, please: read it aloud!"

Everyone will find that sentence and hear it read: as sound.

They have read it silently. This is good for their English.

But reading is all habit. This is just the right brain working.

Now comes the shock to the left!

"Amadeus!" says the teacher. "What do think it means?"

Everyone has heard and has read that sentence. A simple English sentence! But what does it MEAN? You may be asked next.

Suddenly everyone's left brain is working. Amadeus is saying he thinks it means 'this'. Someone disagrees. Another disagrees. You have now had time to decide if you agree or not, and why. You must learn to say this clearly. You must be prepared to be the next to be asked . "Read the next sentence, please. Louder! this time."

It isn't long before the whole class has heard, read, and heard argue, or have argued the meaning of the entire explanation.

The teacher asks, "Are you all happy with this understanding?"

If someone looks doubtful, they should explain why they think it may be faulty. This takes courage. Also confidence.

Everyone will listen. Everyone will decide if they agree.

Notice that the whole class has been involved. Intelligently. No one is made to feel stupid. All their left brains have been active.

All their right brains are prepared to learn something new.

Their teacher has not had been obliged to pretend to teach anything. All that the teacher has done is to make sure that anyone who appears not to be listening is told: "Please read the next line!" Or: "What do *you* think that means?"

The whole class has learnt to listen with attention. To think carefully about meaning. To consider their own opinion. To listen to others' opinions. To decide how to declare their own. To do so clearly. To hear criticism without resentment. To criticize without being offensive.

And beginning to realise they really could do this alone!

Then their teacher tells them turn to the exercises to test the understanding they have agreed to: to choose their own problems to solve, to discover from the answers if their understanding is correct.

This is where the teacher shows confidence in the class.

And they show respect for their teacher.

They made their decision freely.

It was their responsibility alone.

If they find their understanding was faulty, whoever thought something was wrong becomes a hero!

They will all want to suggest how to improve it.

If they find they have solved all problem that they have chosen, their confidence in each other, and in themselves, will be equally as heroic. They will be eager for the next challenge.

This how youngsters everywhere can enjoy learning.

With best wishes from Amadeus.

And the next is my *most* illustrious adventure! I think.

But before you are amazed my last adventure, have you thought how to ask your headteacher and a favourite teacher to let you and your friends try their your first Amadeus lesson?

Tell them you all want to go to college!

School representatives report to AMADEUS (as subject) at educatingmessiahs@gmail.com
National organisers report campaign progress to www.amadeusteaches.com

Amadeus goes to College!

Towards the end of last summer I was invited to Trinity College in Cambridge for one of its regular gatherings. Naturally I wanted to go.

The problem, of course, was Amadeus.

In 1805, when Lord Byron was told to leave his dog at home, he brought a pet bear instead, taking it for a stroll around the grounds every day on a leash.

Amadeus is no longer the puppy I could carry around in an army medic's pouch. He is now six feet long from his nose to the tip of his magnificent tail and he weighs over a hundred pounds. I considered, briefly, declaring him to be a bear.

He is, unmistakeably, a dog.

But there was an alternative. Some of my old maths pupils may remember me sitting entirely unperturbed through the ear-splitting clangour of a fire alarm, and demanding, as the entire class began abruptly to decamp: "Just where the Devil do you think YOU ARE ALL GOING!" And being told, in a delighted chorus: "SIR, THE SCHOOL'S ON FIRE!"

I explained to Trinity's accommodation office that Amadeus is my Hearing Dog. I might be burnt to a crisp unless he slept in my room overnight to warn me of a possible fire. This would reflect badly on the College.

Trinity is not just one of the world's greatest centres of learning, it is also – perhaps even more laudably - astonishingly generous and humane. Amadeus was accepted on just these terms. He would be allowed in my rooms; up to the final bridge leading to the College from the Backs; but not, on pain of being shot, any further into the College itself.

It takes around two hours to drive from Oxford to Cambridge. Late in the evening I was escorted to a beautiful set of modern rooms by the duty porter - carrying the Hearing Dog's blanket. When he asked me whom I hoped to meet the next day, I replied, *"Apart from some American friends, I only know ... "* and named one of Trinity's most eminent scholars, *"... and he will be the only one to know me."*

One can imagine that in Byron's day this somewhat careless reply would have taken forever to reach all the many corners of the College. But as we walked down to the College in the morning, every port᠆ we passed could be heard muttering into his throat mike: *"Here comes the Lord's guest, and his Hearing Dog."*

No one was surprised. And no one took the shot.

Well, I enjoyed my lunch, being seated beside a delightful lady ambassador recently returned from representing Denmark's national interests in Nepal. I also saw my Washington friends. But I saw very little of the fascinating presentations afterwards because I had repeatedly to visit the Hearing Dog in the car park beyond the great iron gates which mark the western boundary of Trinity's immaculate lawns.

This boundary is also marked by a deep ditch, which runs across the Backs from St John's College, past Trinity College, to King's College. It is bridged, at intervals, for vehicles and pedestrians. But to have written 'runs', in the sense of 'flows', is incorrect. It may not have moved an inch sideways since the Magna Carta was signed: 800 years ago this week! It contains a depth of coal-black bacterial sewage in which are floating still identifiable bits of decaying fish and birds. God alone must know, and I write here respectfully, what is underneath.

And, of course, you will know what happened next. Slipping the knot in the rope I had tied to his chain, and as if it were his own Manifest Destiny to get himself repeatedly into nasty situations from which withdrawal is always infinitely more difficult, Amadeus jumped in.

There followed an almost exact reprise of our earlier adventure. At first the same delighted total immersion; then the snapping at the filthy feathers and fragments of fish; then the first attempts to leave; then the discovery that the bank is far too soft; followed by the pitiful whoops and yelps and the beginning of despair.

"*I am ALONE, ALONE, OOH-OOH! A-L-O-N-E!! OOH-OWW!*"

This time, I resolved, I was damned if I was going to get into that ditch with him. I was still hoping to return to my pretty neighbour at lunch. She would not find me so delightful if dripping black slime from the waist down.

But by now Amadeus's whooping and wailing had attracted a flock of foreign tourists who had just debussed from what my Northern primary school headmaster would have called their 'charabang'. Clearly ready to believe that everything in Cambridge is provided for them to be photographed in front of, they were soon snapping shots of a British dog committing a peculiar form of ritual suicide.

Ignoring them, but not without a disdainful glance at this callous audience, two valiant local ladies put down their shopping to haul on one end of the rope whilst I anchored the other, and together we pulled the sodden, stinking, but entirely unremorseful Amadeus out of his horrible ditch.

More tourists arrived. Twittering still more excitedly en masse, they crowded closer. Those in the front rank were holding their cameras near to the ground, whilst those in the second and third had to hold theirs above their heads. Their lenses reflected the scene like so many dark and eager eyes.

I opened my mouth to warn them. Too late! Amadeus was already lowering his head and setting his legs. Once firmly set, and as all dogs do, he commenced to rid his coat of its excess moisture by throwing a perfect penumbra of stinking black ooze, once, twice, three, four times, all over his admirers, their clothes, their spectacles, and their cameras.

Spontaneous cries of joy arose from those in the rear, cries of horror from those in front. "*I really don't think you need wait here any longer, love,"* one of my lady helpers told me, as they both scooped up their shopping and left. I never learnt their names. Thinking this also wise, I made a tactical withdrawal to a position well within Trinity's gate, where I paused beside a silent but clearly sympathetic porter to assess this new situation.

A two-hour drive back to Oxford? Even in the open air, the stink rising from Amadeus was appalling. In the car it would be unbearable. The car itself would have to be written off. What to do?

Obviously, put him back – no, not into the ditch: into the gentle Cam, into the clean and gentle Cam, flowing across the Backs, beneath so many pretty clean bridges, carrying so many beautiful *clean* young people.

But how? Arriving at the bank, just before the bridge into the College

I was not allowed to cross with him, my heart sank. As you will see, the bank had been revetted to a height of two feet. I could get him in, but to lift him out?

"Can I help?" said an angel, a beautiful young lady, in black and white uniform clothes, clearly of great compassion, generosity, and virtue, who suddenly appeared beside me. Later I realized that she had also been summoned - wirelessly - by my guardians in their bowler hats.

"I'm Jess," she told me. *"And isn't he,"* referring now to the reeking lump of sodden fur that I had tied to a tree at our feet, "s-o-o *beautiful!"* Amadeus blinked at her as if his present state of squalor was a mystery to him. *"I shall get Mr Shanahan,"* breathed the angel. *"He will know just what to do."*

In the employ of P. G. Wodehouse's creation, Lord Emsworth, Beach, his magnificent butler, is frequently reported to have the ability, very much like that of the famous Indian guru Sai Baba, of being able to materialise out of empty air; and even of bi-location, of appearing in two places at once.

I now learnt that Mr Cornelius Shanahan, the Catering Manager of Trinity College, Cambridge, is able to do this too: possibly while still supervising his staff back in the splendid surroundings of the Wren Library and Neville's Court.

"Good afternoon, Sir," said Mr Cornelius, as Jess always called him, materialising beside me out of the empty air. *"Allow me to suggest that we take your dog to the punt slipway to wash him clean there with a borrowed hose."*

"But," I responded feebly, hardly recovered from the shock of his sudden appearance, *"I can't go over there."*

"Then I", Mr Shanahan majestically declared, *"shall escort you myself!"*

And he did. Led by brave Jessica, careless of her shiny black pumps, her immaculate skirt and her crisp white blouse, all already showing multiple signs of the Hearing Dog's affection, and followed by your humble servant, we proceeded to the punt slipway, at the corner of the College grounds, where a crowd of happy tourists were being slotted into place in punts, like sardines.

Our appearance created a stir.

Mr Cornelius explained his desires to the young men in charge. They began at once to move their punts out of the way. When I looked again to where he had been, not a shadow of Cornelius Shanahan remained.

But there was no time to lose. The walkway beside the basin being too narrow for all three of us, Jessica passed Amadeus to me, who immediately displayed the fatheaded misconception common to celebrities everywhere that his idiot antics were being applauded by all right-thinking people.

He stopped at the edge of the dock to wag his tail in response to the cheers of his audience in the punts in midstream. With something approaching the emotion of one called upon to betray a simple-minded but still trusting friend, I applied my right foot to his bum and pushed him, very briskly, into the Cam. There was a still greater cheer from his audience as he broke surface, puffing in the midst of a great spreading black stain, as much of the filth from the ditch washed off him at once. By the time he swam back to the slip, he was clean. Everyone, this time, stood clear of the deluge.

I never got to thank Jess properly, if at all. She disappeared too. Perhaps one day I hope that she - and Mr Shanahan - will see this and receive my heartfelt thanks; as I hope the nearly invisible but highly efficient troop of bowler-hatted gentlemen who brought them to my - that is, to our - aid will also.

Thanks to you all.

And of course, by the time I returned to the luncheon, it was over. The Danish ambassador left no note.

I tried finally to find my Washington friends in the college where they usually stay, but they had also disappeared.

In the end, therefore, this must be

the End

Grief is a very personal madness. And perhaps I should be ashamed to feel so much for the death of 'just a dog'. But it can also be productive: by making apparent what is really important in one's life. Learning from a dog, for example, the honesty, sincerity, courage and simplicity that is natural to their kind. I therefore include this final letter to my own ex-pupils and others, to explain to the teachers and parents I may never meet just how serious is the real purpose of this book. I really have written it with the help of the presence of my dear friend, Amadeus. I want your children to enjoy his adventures, and for his life to continue in their memory, as it will in mine. But this is for you. Having been a soldier, I began teaching at Magdalen College School in Oxford. Later, as head of mathematics of the first official European School in Britain, near Oxford, I was able to develop and apply the method of teaching my pupils to learn that Amadeus describes. Within seven years my junior pupils became my senior students, consistently achieving amongst the highest grades in the European Baccalaureate of all the then thirteen European Schools. Many of them are still in touch with me, thirty and forty years later. To the immense benefit of millions of young people, and later their societies, all schools could use this method: and not only in mathematics! If they won't, perhaps it will because of the scornful question I was once asked in a major conference in Europe: "Do you really suppose our governments want us to teach children to think?" Only the children can insist that this is precisely what they want from their schools. Yes, they do want to learn to think!

Dear Friends,

This is the fourth day since Amadeus died. What follows may be hard for you to read, but I need you to know how close I have been to dying, to accompany him, to accept the wonderful nature of the inspiration that has arisen from it.

Its consequence has been described before by far greater men: most recently by Einstein; two thousand years ago by Jesus. What no one appears to have noticed before is that Jesus's rules for entering the Kingdom of God are the same as the rules for democracy.

It took the shock of Amadeus' death to shake me sufficiently to see this.

I buried him myself, you see. As soon as it was possible to wake a neighbour, he helped carry him to my car and I drove to the farm where my two friends had agreed years before, in case of need, that he could be buried on their land.

I explained my need, with some difficulty. There was no discussion. The one gentle man that looked at the other, then nodded. "I'll get it done by lunchtime."

I drove home again to collect Amadeus' toys, and when I returned the digger was groaning and straining to excavate his grave. When it was ready, I placed the pink rug that he used to lie on in the car on the bottom of the pit, and was helped to carry him to it.

I lay him on his left side, as he always liked to lie, and arranged his old friend Koko, the stuffed gorilla with which he used to battle as a puppy at his head, and his two small teddy bears beside him. Then I covered him with the big soft brown woollen blanket that was under the rug, then I knelt down and kissed his dear white cheek as soft and smooth as as velvet. And covered him with the blanket.

I stood at one side as the grave was filled. *"I'll tidy it up when it's settled,"* he told me/ *"This has been a kindness beyond anything I can express thanks for,"* I told him.

He held out his big strong sunburnt hand. *"Not at all,"* was his reply.

And it was over.

But, of course it is not over. For three days and nights I have been teetering on the age of a void, filled alternately with horror, disbelief, anger, and guilt.

Guilt, most of all, that I failed him.

Amadeus died of the kind of pernicious anaemia not uncommon in his breed. The heat made it worse. My attempts to help him take his pills were not helpful. If I had not left him alone, he might have died in my arms, but die he would, and did.

I have told of that moment when, I believe, as he died, his spirit joined with mine. But trying to stay sane carrying this burden of grief, I have found, is very hard. With every breath I feel as if I am about to lose my balance and slip into the darkness. And the truth is that this would be welcome, an end, a quietus. To join him, up there, somewhere, nowhere. At least no longer to be alone.

It has been in these moments that I discovered something truly miraculous.

I didn't usually call him Amadeus. This was more his title, rather than his name. Usually I called him 'Babe'. And so, as I find myself teetering on the edge of the void, I take a quick breath and tell to him: *"Stay with me, Babe."*

It is still hard. He grew and shed hairs as if this was his sole purpose in life, and, of course, his hairs are everywhere. Every one I find, especially on me, I must take another quick breath and say: *"Don't go, Babe, stay with me."*

I keep on doing all the inconsequential things a house and home require. Writing helps too: for I can write a line, and stop, and write another line and stop. And I find an email from the Carnegie Foundation inviting my contribution to 'a future in which educational leaders together make meaningful, measurable improvements on the longstanding disparities in students' progress through our nation's schools.'

Hmm. But aren't these 'leaders' also responsible for the meaningful, measurable, disastrous present, the present that they are now supposed to improve?

Schools are the breeding grounds of all the insanities that blight our societies, that divide and weaken nations, that bring war and destruction to other societies, that threaten to destroy us entirely. Hopes for a unity of humankind that any god worth the name should demand, are everywhere swept aside by human vanity, arrogance, greed, spite, and cruelty. We are creating these faults through 'education'.

It is now late evening. I don't remember having eaten anything since burying him, but I am remembering replying to a kind note from another friend in Cambridge, telling him of the moment when I asked aloud: *"How could one puncture the vanity of these hopeless nonentities?"* And that new low gruff voice answered: *"Bite 'em."*

This wasn't me.

Bite 'em? But how bite 'em?

And suddenly it came to me, and again I said aloud, amazed: *"Babe, that how to do it! We need an Amadeus Project! We must tell the kids directly what they are missing!"*

He never said 'Bite hard'. Amadeus was a strategical thinker. He would wake me in the early hours by sticking his big cold wet nose in my ear and snuffling anxiously.

But do of those 'educational leaders' ever give a moment's attention to the disastrous spiritual damage caused by treating the minds of their pupils like so many empty buckets, their success or their failure in exams like the profit or loss of their stocks and shares?

"And said I say unto you, except ye be converted, and become as little children, ye shall not enter into the kingdom of heaven."

The language is gentle. The message is ferocious. And still more direct: "I came not to send peace, but a sword."

Would his sword be to separate the children of his time from their spiritually destructive teachers: 'the teachers of laws and worshippers of dead bones'?

Those teachers hated him. He despised them: *"You hypocrites who shut the kingdom of heaven against others, knowing nothing of it, yet preventing them from entering."*

Realizing that they were usually fed on rancid slops, the common people flocked to hear him. Instead of taking their money for meaningless prayers and rituals, he challenged them prove their spiritual strength themselves. They should look to their own faults, and forgive others. Should treat others as deserving the same respect as themselves. Should expect others to do the same. Listen to their argument, compare them with their own. Not spit at their feet in derision.

This was dangerously subversive! How could he be stopped?

I have felt the spit of modern hypocrites. They cannot admit that their methods of teaching are the cause of their society's division, national weakness, its spiritual despair. A recent modern fad is to teach 'critical thinking'. But every kind of extremism is based on critical thinking: of others' beliefs, not one's own. What is required is not to be critical, this is easy; but to join in constructive engagement.

This requires a totally different set of mind: as we can understand it now, of intelligent left brain thinking instead of emotional right brain reaction.

This is what that inspired man was warning the Jews two thousand years ago would happen. If they had only listened, their nation might not have been destroyed.

Our societies, our nations, are being weakened the same way. I remember always that question at the conference in Germany: "Do you really suppose that *our* governments want us to teach their children *to think*?" This generally amused.

I remember the deputy school director who visited my lesson with some fourteen year-olds, telling me, after the class had left: "You must stop teaching your pupils like this at once: *or in another few years they won't need a teacher at all!"*

I sat back in wonder, having only realizing just now that what Jesus was explaining. It was both spiritual *and* political: how to create democracy, and keep it strong. For a very modest outlay we can tell children ourselves.

How's that to bite 'em?

"Babe," I told him, *"We've done it. I mean, YOU'VE done it."*

The elation was real. It still is real. Has anyone in all of the past two thousand years recognised this is what he meant? The bitterness remains. Had it to cost so much?

Finally to bed, still murmuring from time to time, 'Stay with me, Babe. Stay with me." For the first time not feeling so utterly alone.

For two days I have been terrified of attempting to sleep. Usually I would have to step over Amadeus in the dark. And so, as usual, I warn him, *"Watch out, Amadeus, I'm stepping over you."*

I have been talking to him like this for two days. It saves me from the terror of noticing that he is not there. Now I have the Babe to listen to me.

"We've no need to be invited to any 'Education Summit'. We can create a handbook right here. Just a few pages, quite slim. For parents, and kids and their

teachers. To tell them how to keep the kids in their school from being made to believe they are first-rate, and the most deserving; or second-rate, and disappointing, or third-rate damaged goods."

All of them learning to hate and distrust one another. This is as Einstein realized was beginning to happen when he wrote, in 1949: *'An exaggerated competitive attitude is inculcated in students trained to worship only acquisitive success. Our entire education system suffers from this evil. The solution is teach them to work and to think together.'*

That's also my memory. I think he wrote 'oriented to social goals'.

Like many scientists of his era, he must have thought 'social goals' would mean not treating people as cattle.

But this this happens when any school treats children as cattle.

Just as dangerous is the emphasis in science on truth. In my play that I wrote as a young soldier: about Jesus before Pilate; when Pilate asks his famous question, *"What is truth?"* Jesus only smiles, inclining his head to indicate his answer: 'That question.'

"We can do this" I told the Babe. *"Tomorrow."* And fell thankfully asleep.

Today is the fifth day. I am still sad. But now I have the Babe with me. And now we have a plan to save millions of children from being persuaded by their soul-destroying education that they should fear, or pity, or despise other children, and when adults, feel the same of whole classes of other people.

Two thousand years ago Jesus told that the way to entering the Kingdom of God is by exploring the reality of unconditional love, forgiveness, and trust.

And although the Jews would never recognize it, he was also describing how to create a democracy, and keep it, and its nation, strong. Even democracy can be helped by this.

First we must insist that their schools stop teaching children to compete for the right to look with that pity, or derision, or contempt on any who succeed less well, nor to envy and dislike those who leave them behind.

By everyone learning to work together, achieving and sharing their success together, everyone becoming more individual and more confident. They can then begin to recognize what the Kingdom of God should look like here on Earth.

How simple! The kids will love lessons like these.

If only they could tell my dear Amadeus. Although I now feel his spirit within me, his physical loss is still a weight on my heart. He should be lying beside me right now, looking up occasionally: 'I can see you are busy. But when can we go out?'

First it must have an arresting title:

AMADEUS TEACHES

Under that one of your best photos.

And under that: *'Learn together, stay strong.'*

"Tomorrow," I told him, "we do the inside."

Colin Hannaford, Oxford, UK, 9th -16th July 2018.

This was all written, as you have seen, within two weeks of Amadeus' death.

The pain this caused was astonishing; but I wanted others to know of the happiness I have known in his presence; and to understand why I should feel ready to do *anything* to bring him back. It was this that made me ask: what might others feel that they have lost, and feel ready to do *anything* to bring it back?

Many years ago I noticed a question in a philosophy exam for the senior French pupils. 'Describe the cause of existential anguish.' I shrugged: very French. I had no idea what existential anguish might mean. Now I think I do.

For many millions it is must be to realise that they were never given the right opportunity to learn to work intelligently with others. They were always expected to obey and compete, obey and compete; no sympathy for losers; expecting none when they themselves fail; to despise all other people seen as inadequate, or 'different'.

Here is surely the cause of epidemic depression in many societies. It may even be that endless preparation for wars is a distraction from this same anguish.

If his little book of advice and adventures can help children to bring the habit of constructive engagement to the world, instead of envy, hatred, and violence, it will be a fitting memorial to Amadeus, and all his kind.

*

It is now one month later, the sadness is less, the 'presence of the absent', as a kind friend described it, is much the same. To discourage the notion that I am just a mad old man grieving for his dog, it has been helpful for people to learn that I was the first to describe plainly, twenty years ago, the connection between mathematics and democracy; that I have received an award for this in the United States; have been nominated for a Canadian Peace Prize; have published and lectured in Europe, America, and the Middle East on how to teach mathematics more effectively in schools. Nothing important followed. It was as if I and my friends were suggesting that a 'basket of deplorables' should replace all political elites. Instead of gradual change the basket of deplorables became the Islamic State: chaos followed.

Especially encouraging now is to be noticed by the Oxford Mail, and that a famous Oxford bookshop, Blackwell's, has taken our book to display: at first only to give it away, later to sell. Since its many hundreds of summer visitors will be looking for a special Oxford souvenir, I suggested that this should attract their attention:

**'CHILDREN OF THE WORLD:
REFUSE TO BE TAUGHT TO HATE OTHERS!'**

'Oh, how the love of God causes us to hate,' was the lament of a famous Oxford don. There are many teachers of hatred in the world. In China, in contrast, an immensely long experience of history is expressed through an emphasis on four 'pillars' of education: *'learning to know, learning to do, learning to live together, learning to be.'*

All learning requires the left brain. All aggression is directed by the right brain. Young people everywhere should know this. Directing the right brain to reject its own most destructive emotion is a step towards peace for all humankind.

I learnt this from Amadeus' dying. I wish this had not been the reason.

R.I.P.

FROM DIVIDED TRIBES
TO FIRST NATION

'The development of a rational, innovative society, internally harmonious and tolerant of dissent, depends on understanding the historic connection between learning mathematics as argument and democracy.'

OU Philosophical Society Essay Prize, 1995.

PRAISE FROM AMERICA

"I think you are onto something!"

Professor Noam Chomsky, MIT, 1996.

FROM EUROPE

"You have made an important contribution to the intellectual, moral, and social understanding of our world."

Professor Freiherr C. F. von Weizsaecker, 1997.

FROM CANADA

'His proposal for the reform of mathematics education is radical and profound'.

Nomination for Canadian Parliament Peace Prize, 1998.

FROM AMERICA

"When we teach mathematics as an adventure of intelligence that they share with all the people on Earth, we teach confidence, freedom, respect for others and generosity. If instead we show them limitation; teach subordination instead of confidence; obedience, instead of generosity, we are not educating our pupils to be citizens but to be subjects: as most governments prefer."

Quoted in US Association for Curriculum Development handbook, 2007.

FROM OXFORD:

'The *manner* in which students are taught to learn will shape what they value and how they relate to and treat other people. Mathematics can be taught in such a fashion as to foster the love of victory and domination, and the vices of competitive selfishness, dissembling, conformism, and resentment. Alternatively it can be taught to encourage the love of the truth, the virtues of collaboration, honesty, and critical inquisitiveness. I encourage serious consideration of this important project'

Professor Nigel Biggar, Christ Church, 2010.

FROM CAMBRIDGE:

'charming, educational, inspirational'

Professor Lord Martin Rees FRS, Trinity College, 2018.

89182288R00018

Made in the USA
San Bernardino, CA
21 September 2018